The
Gu
Inclusion

Philip Douch

The Buskers Guide to Inclusion

ISBN 978-1-904792-15-4

With grateful thanks to our pre-publication 'readers';
Christina Downey - SEN/Disabilities Co-ordinator (Out of School Provision),
Disabled Children's Services, Northampton County Council
Liz Carroll - Inclusive Play Co-ordinator, zero14plus (DEYDCP),
Devon Early Years Development and Childcare Partnership

Published by Common Threads Publications Ltd. *in association with*
Wessex House
Upper Market Street
Eastleigh
Hampshire SO50 9FD
T: 02380 629460
E: info@commonthreads.org.uk
W: www.commonthreads.org.uk

Other titles in The Buskers Guide series include:
The Buskers Guide to Playwork
The Buskers Guide to Behaviour
The Buskers Guide to Playing Out
The Buskers Guide to Anti-Discriminatory Practice
The Buskers Guide to Risk
The Buskers Guide to Participation
The Big Buskers Guide to Leadership

The text of 'The Buskers Guide...' series can be made available in 14 point font - please contact the publishers by telephoning 02380 629460 or emailing info@commonthreads.org.uk

The Buskers Guide to Inclusion

Contents

Introduction

I guess I owe quite a lot to Graham. When I was 16 I went on a week's holiday with a group of disabled children. I can only recall ever having met one disabled person before that week. Fortunately, Graham confounded any stereotypes.

After his mum had been prescribed the thalidomide drug during pregnancy, Graham had been born with such short limbs that he had, in effect, flippers for arms and legs. Outdoors he used a wheelchair; indoors he shuffled across the floor at alarming speed on his bum, periodically over-balancing and shouting, 'Pick me up!' at the nearest available fully-armed bystander. And off he'd go again until the next nose dive.

When he was out with us one day, two boys did the classic stop and stare stuff, one saying to the other, 'Why's that boy got such little arms and such little legs?' To which Graham impressively replied, 'Why've you got such a bloody big mouth?'

I didn't realise it at the time, but Graham and his mates that week set me on a path that led to lots of work supporting disabled children's right to play – and also set me off with a pretty healthy attitude to disability. Lots of other people have shaped that attitude in the thirty years post-Graham, and I've tried to share what I've learned by promoting inclusion through the work of Kids. So it's great to have the chance to reach a few more people now by being invited to write this Buskers Guide.

Sometimes when I get to speak at conferences I ask how many participants have already included disabled children in their settings. Typically perhaps a third to a half of the people present raise their hands. If I ask how many of these found it really difficult, most of the hands go down. Then, if I ask those with their hands still up whether it was worth going through the difficulties, nearly everyone reckons it was. So, I say to them all – as I say to you now as you read this – why aren't we all doing it?

I think the answer is basically in four parts.

First, we aren't all including disabled children because it would take some extra time and effort. I don't mean this as a criticism. Not many people working with children have much of either to spare.

Second, our personal lives have probably not given most of us the opportunity to know many disabled people.

Third, our professional lives have encouraged us to think of disabled children as having 'special needs' – so they go to special places with special staff who presumably have special skills that ordinary workers don't possess.

And fourth, largely as a consequence of the second and third things above, we're apprehensive/frightened/terrified (circle your own level of panic as appropriate). We are legitimately concerned that we won't know what to do and that we won't be able to provide a properly professional service.

All of these explanations seem to me to be perfectly reasonable, but it's interesting that the same factors probably hold true for many of the people who *are* including disabled children as well as for those who aren't.

So what's the key ingredient? Why does inclusion happen in some places and not in others? I think it's fundamentally pretty simple. Inclusion happens where people believe in it – where they really want it to happen. It becomes successful where everyone has a positive can-do attitude and when people truly work together for everyone's benefit.

There is no special set of extra skills involved. In fact there's nothing 'special' going on at all. Inclusion is just good practice. It is spectacularly ordinary – though the impact may be quite profound. In years to come, when inclusion happens routinely, I hope people will find this Buskers Guide rather quaint. 'How strange!' they will say, 'Why ever did he have to write that? Of course that's what we do. It's just common sense.'

Philip Douch

Chapter 1
What is inclusion?

There are loads of definitions of inclusion. Some are
related specifically to disabled children and their
involvement in ordinary life; others to the involvement
of all children, whatever their backgrounds or
characteristics may be. This Buskers Guide focuses
mainly on disabled children, but I think it'll soon become
apparent that the inclusive principles which emerge are
universally applicable.

Whose problem?
Let's start with disability. Most of us have grown up with
the idea that disability is something someone's 'got' –
Maurice has 'got cerebral palsy'; Boris has 'got autism';
Doris is blind and has therefore 'got a disability'. It's like
it belongs to them and they carry it round with them all
the time – and it causes them all sorts of problems
because it means they can't do some things very easily.

This is the definition contained in the 1995 Disability
Discrimination Act, which calls disability a 'physical or
mental impairment which has a substantial and long-
term adverse effect on a person's ability to carry out

normal day-to-day activities'. It locates the problem squarely with the individual. It sometimes even leads us to ask 'what's wrong' with someone – which is a rather offensive question when you think about it.

However, there's another way altogether of looking at disability – and it's the way in which many disabled people themselves choose to understand their experience. Whilst they freely acknowledge that they've got some sort of impairment, they ask us to recognise that many of the problems they face don't come from their impairments at all. In fact the difficulties arise from the discrimination they face in a world that refuses to accept that it's perfectly ordinary for some people to have these impairments.

Design our streets, buildings and transport differently, and a wheelchair-user will still have an impairment but will no longer be disabled by steps and inaccessible vehicles. Stop treating disabled people as weirdos or heroes, and they will no longer be disabled by our attitudes towards them. Review the policies we have which inadvertently inhibit disabled people's right to take part in things, and they will no longer be disabled by organisational barriers. Give away professional power and control over disabled people's lives, and they will no longer be disabled by being prevented from making choices about their own lives.

Our responsibility

This way of looking at disability removes the problem from the individual with an impairment and puts it firmly with how the rest of us respond to people who have those impairments. It's not their problem; it's our responsibility.

For those of you who like a bit of theory with your Buskers Guide, the first way of looking at disability – focused on people's impairments – is usually described

as the medical model. The second way – focused on the barriers and discrimination they face – is called the social model. A neat shorthand way of remembering the difference is that the medical model concentrates on the person's 'condition', whilst the social model emphasises the 'conditions' under which they experience their daily lives.

There is only a limited amount that can be done about the medical stuff, and it's mostly specialists who can do it. But there is masses that can be done about the social stuff, and each and every one of us can help to make a difference.

Well, I hear you say, this is all very interesting (or not, depending on your love of impressive theory), but what has it got to do with how we work with children? And back comes my reply, 'Everything! (or at least a heck of a lot).' Because we'll actually approach the way we work with disabled children quite differently depending on how we understand disability – even if we aren't conscious that we're doing so.

If we have a medical model perspective, we may well focus on what a child's got. Our concern will be to take care of the child, look after her, and make sure she's safe. All of this is perfectly fine of course. I am not about to discredit myself by suggesting that we shouldn't be taking care of disabled kids! We should be taking care of any child we work with. But it is only a starting point.

Keeping children safe is surely only a means to a greater end. With non-disabled children we do make sure they're safe of course, but don't we have a greater, bolder, more exciting set of aims in mind? Stuff like fun,

adventure, risk, laughter, challenge? And so it must be for disabled children too – *especially* for disabled children, in fact. Otherwise, in our proper concern to ensure they're safe, being safe is all we'll offer them.

If we bring social model understandings to what we do, we won't just see disabled kids as a batch of medical problems in need of careful management. Instead we'll be passionate about removing the barriers and challenging the assumptions that disadvantage them. We'll do all we can to eliminate these negative experiences that effectively turn 'children with impairments' into 'disabled children'. We'll take due account of what they've got, but our prime intention will be to offer them the fullest range of choices – *en*abling, rather than *dis*abling, them by all that we do.

Key features of inclusion

This leads us neatly on to what I mean by inclusion. It's about disabled children – in fact all children - having the widest choices possible and being able to exercise those choices in whatever ways work for them. It's about all of us sharing an attitude of welcome, respect and responsiveness. It entails participation and belonging.

Inclusion is not just about herding a big mix of children into the same place. I guess most of us have been to parties where there's been a big mix of people but where we have personally felt anything but included. It is as easy to be isolated in a crowd as anywhere else.

What we need at the party is to be genuinely welcomed, to feel we have as much right to be there as anyone else, and – if necessary – for our host or fellow party-goers to look out for us and help us to feel at ease in whatever way we may need. In short, we want to feel like we belong. And we will only feel like that if we feel like someone is interested in each one of us who's there.

So inclusion is principally about relationships. Ramps, toilets and policies may all be important, but a setting is only as inclusive as the people who welcome you into it. And this is where you come in, dear reader! The welcome and the respectful relationships are down to you.

It's ok to be nervous

But before we go any further, let's acknowledge that feeling some level of uncertainty about including disabled children is perfectly normal. It is, in fact, the logical outcome of a society and a history that has traditionally sent disabled kids off to a 'special' place somewhere else.

I'm not suggesting that this has been done in the past because people wanted to be nasty to disabled children, but there are some inevitable consequences. One of which is that if we don't routinely bump into disabled children from our earliest years growing up; if they are bussed off to different schools and excluded from places other people go and if you then need to have separate training to work with them, people will inevitably find themselves feeling nervous about taking responsibility for children they are not familiar with.

So, any apprehension is only to be expected. You won't get any condemnation from me for ignorance (literally 'not knowing'). It's not anyone's fault if you feel a bit wobbly; and the longer you haven't worked with disabled children, the more likely the change is going to feel a bit threatening. It is quite usual for ignorance to lead to fear, but we then need to prevent our fear leading to prejudice. And the best way to prevent this is to address our ignorance - by meeting some disabled people and getting to know them.

We can do this for ourselves by making that time and effort to welcome them into our setting. And in doing so we will also be creating another benefit, because we will be giving an opportunity to all the children we work with that was probably denied to us – a chance to be in a place where disabled and non-disabled children grow up thinking it's perfectly ordinary to be together.

The Three P's

WOW!

As I mentioned in the introduction, 'ordinary' is a key word in this book. You might notice that it contrasts rather sharply with 'special'. This is because I don't think it does anyone any good to think of some children as 'special'. As far as I'm concerned, either all children are special or none are. Once we start identifying a sub-section as somehow *particularly* special, I think a whole load of unhelpful attitudes tend to creep in — summed up rather neatly in what I call 'the three P's'.

You've probably seen the three P's in cringe-inducing action. First, disabled children can get patronised — otherwise known as 'pat-the-brave-little-darling-on-the-head syndrome'. Second, they can get pitied - 'oh, it must be awful - it's such a shame she's confined to that wheelchair'. And third, at the other end of the scale, they can find themselves placed on pedestals for triumphing over supposed adversity – 'wow, he's just amazing; I could never do what he's done'.

None of this is going to help disabled children's view of themselves. Nor is it any good for non-disabled children's understanding. We need to be having the same

quality of relationship with disabled kids as the non-disabled ones. Which does not mean it's all going to be dreadfully po-faced and stilted and correct. It means we'll treat everyone like human beings, having a laugh as well as taking notice of whatever they may need.

I hope the point is pretty clear by now that, despite our history's worst efforts to convince us otherwise, disabled kids are not another species from the planet Zarg.

They're kids, with the same fundamental needs and wide range of individual interests as other kids. How those needs are best met will vary from child to child of course – but then they do with non-disabled children too.

You can do it!

So let's de-mythologise a bit. If you are good at working with children, you can be good at working with a few more. Good practice is good practice. And inclusive practice is just making conscious and deliberate many of the things we do, or should be doing, anyway.

In fact one of the real advantages of including disabled children in your work is that it will frequently remind you of how you should be working with *all* children. You will come across just the same issues as you do with other children, only sometimes the presence of a disabled child will make you see the issue more obviously; you'll see the same stuff but you'll see it bigger. So, from your setting's point of view, welcoming disabled children is likely to promote even better quality in your work – which can't be bad, can it?

And from disabled children's point of view - well, they're getting their rights to choose things in their community just as other children can, which can't be bad either.

Some time in the future - and we can all do our bit to shorten the time this takes to happen – no newspaper will think it worth reporting that 'brave little Boris, despite suffering from spina bifida, has been taken in by the kind-hearted staff at his local playgroup and is making a terrific go of it.' (There we go, the three P's beautifully encapsulated in a single piece of newspaper-ese — patronising, pity and pedestal).

No, this should not be a news story. The kid at number 13 Acacia Avenue goes to the playgroup. The kid at number 17 goes there too. And Boris lives at number 15, so of course he goes there if he wants to. Unremarkable. Ordinary.

Chapter 2
How do we practise inclusion?

Beliefs and attitudes

Even if we aren't aware of it, our practice is inevitably driven by what we believe. For inclusion to work, we need a fundamental belief that disabled children have the same right to be in our provision as anyone else. When I was looking for a school for my own (non-disabled) son, I came across one school's information for parents that said some disturbingly bizarre things. They said they were 'very willing to accept children who are handicapped' because this provided their 'own children' with experience of other less fortunate ones.

It's a depressing but perfect example of what can happen when disabled children are taken out of the mainstream of our society and then re-inserted; they are not even seen to be 'our own children'.

So, before I say anything about how we actually practice inclusion, I have to stress once again that the key to our

practice – to what we do and how we do it – is what we believe about disabled children and their involvement in our provision. I've already tried to get rid of the idea that we're just going to keep them 'safe'. I'd also like to uncover any half-hidden notions that we're somehow doing them a favour by letting them come to our provision – that 'we are very willing to accept' them (what grudging words!).

Inclusion means that each child will be positively welcomed, not merely accepted. And every single one will have as much right to be there as the next one. You won't be 'integrating' one group of children into another group of children. This suggests there's some kind of 'them and us' going on. In inclusion there is only 'us'.

We also need to avoid the situation where children have a 'trial period' to see if they 'fit in'. What does it do to a child to be put on trial for who they are? Either a setting is open to everyone or it's not! Parent, child and setting may occasionally come to the joint conclusion that this is not where Boris wants to be, but that is very different from being told his impairments mean he isn't welcome. Rather than trying to make the children fit the setting, the setting needs to fit around its children.

Welcome and respect

At the heart of good inclusive practice there is a genuine commitment to welcome each person. This is not reserved for 'special' children (from the planet Zarg); it's how you are with all the children. Nor is it just about the children. It's about the quality of every relationship you have, whether with children, parents, staff, volunteers or other professionals – with the person who delivers the milk, drives the minibus or turns up looking for directions to the library. Where there is real concern for people, inclusion is likely to follow. Where there isn't, it won't.

Reasonable adjustments

Let's go back to the Disability Discrimination Act for a little while. Earlier on I moaned about its definition of disability focusing only on the medical model, but its actual requirements do also reflect an understanding of the social model. At its core the Act requires that anyone providing any sort of service must not discriminate against disabled people. And it demands that we make 'reasonable adjustments' – i.e. we must do everything we can to fit around disabled peoples' needs, rather than just merrily carrying on as if they didn't exist.

Think of it this way. You have a friend coming to stay for the weekend who is a vegetarian. You and your family are raging omnivores, rarely eating any meal without a good slab of dead animal. So what do you do when your friend comes to visit? Sit him down to dinner each evening just as if he was one of the family because you don't want to treat him any differently – first night roast beef, second night pork casserole? No, of course you don't. You want to welcome him. You respect the fact that he is different from you in some ways, and taking account of these differences is one way in which you demonstrate that he really is welcome in your home.

What you do is to make 'reasonable adjustments'. These might take a number of forms. If he has no problem with meat as long as it's on someone else's plate rather than his, you may simply serve him the roast without the beef – taking care not to do the potatoes in the meat pan. You might decide to do some extra veg or to cook an alternative to the beef. One good way of reaching a decision about all of this would be to talk to him in advance.

Similarly, you might want to establish whether the mere sight of meat makes him uncomfortable. If so, you might reach the conclusion that this weekend is a good opportunity to try out the bean casserole and a variety of salads. Maybe he can even recommend something he really likes and teach you how to make it?

And if he comes to stay for the whole summer rather than just the weekend, what will you do for your meat fix? Well, you could discuss the situation with him and work out arrangements you could all feel okay with – perhaps you won't always eat together or you'll each put up with occasional meals that aren't ideal, or you'll focus most of your carnivorous activities at lunchtimes when he's out.

Essentially you all give each other the respect you deserve, making adjustments accordingly, and working out together what will work best for all of you. Sounds a bit like another definition of inclusion.

Policies, practices and procedures

Since the law says that we must make these 'reasonable adjustments' to our buildings, lots of people assume that it's all about ramps and door widths. In fact, the heart of the Disability Discrimination Act (or the DDA as I shall now refer to it) is about 'policies, practices and procedures'. It simply requires us to respect disabled people and to demonstrate such respect in practice - by changing the ways we do things if what we've done in the past would cause difficulties to a disabled person.

So, if you tend to leave toys scattered all over the floor, you may need a different regime if a blind child joins your group. And his sense of belonging may not exactly be reinforced if, just when he has worked out where everything is kept, you disturb his world by moving it all around. Similarly, if you have a child with learning

difficulties who has a tendency to run away, you may need to think about the effectiveness of your doors or gates and you may need to re-consider the way you allocate supervision responsibilities to staff.

With all this emphasis on reasonable adjustments, you probably won't be surprised to hear that the DDA is not too keen on blanket policies affecting all disabled children. For instance, it's not a good idea to make statements like 'Our building is not suitable for disabled children'. Why? Because what you really mean is, 'We have a flight of six steps to our play space.' Not all disabled children use wheelchairs — in fact well under 10% are wheelchair users — so most disabled children could certainly access your building.

And what about those who do use wheelchairs? Some may be outraged that you meet in a building without ramped access - even though you are planning to change this in the future if possible - and will decide you're not for them. Others may feel that you're so welcoming that they volunteer to shuffle upstairs on their bottoms, despite the indignity, because it's worth it once they get there. Others may be happy to be lifted, either in or out of the chair, just as long as you work out how this can be done safely for you and for them — and that you have an agreed method for getting them downstairs if there is an emergency.

We should note in passing here that disabled people are not 'fire hazards' (in fact, they are no more likely to spontaneously combust than anyone else....).

Toilets!

A word here about toilets too – often a source of difficulty but too often an excuse for excluding disabled children. In the long term (for existing buildings) and in the short term (for new buildings), securing accessible toilets, with space to wash and change teenagers as well as younger children, should be the aim. Meanwhile we have to push for improved facilities and also make the best of what we've got at the moment. In reality (though regrettably), many disabled children do not even have proper facilities in their own homes, and they and their families have to work out ways of managing.

If your setting is genuinely welcoming and really wants to do whatever it reasonably can, then there will usually be a way you can work out what to do, together with the child and parent. It won't perhaps be perfect, but it may well be good enough until such time as you can make it better. And on the rare occasions when nothing you can come up with seems acceptable, at least the experience for child and parent is that everyone has listened and tried to help, rather than simply excluding them.

By the way, it is not compatible with the DDA for a setting to have a policy that requires children to be continent before they can attend. This would effectively deny the chance of attending pre-school, nursery or indeed playscheme or after-school club to any child whose impairment happened to mean they had no bladder or bowel control. This is clearly unfair. Once again, the provision must consider the situation of the

individual child and discuss whatever adjustments could reasonably be made.

I sometimes mischievously ask early years providers if they've ever had a child 'have an accident', and whether they then send him home if he does. Everyone has had this happen, of course, and nobody sends the child home. They find a way of responding — usually involving a store of spare clothes, a member of staff sensitively cleaning up and changing the child, and so on. Then how much easier it would be for you, I suggest, if you actually knew that this would happen with a particular child and could discuss with child, parents, colleagues, support staff and advisers how best to make arrangements in advance, rather than having to respond when it happens unexpectedly (which, in fact, you have actually managed perfectly well....).

One child I know has a vibrating alarm watch she wears at after-school club, reminding her every hour to take herself off to the toilet. Other settings identify a need for an extra adult and access this support through local authority inclusion grants. There may occasionally still be circumstances where acceptable arrangements cannot be made, but it's unusual for no reasonable adjustments to be possible if everyone adopts a 'can-do' attitude.

'Can-do' attitudes

And what is true for bodily functions is true for pretty much everything else relating to disabled children! That is, if practitioners approach each situation negatively, feeling put upon by this annoying legislation that requires them to 'accept' children they shouldn't have to, then life will be hard and they won't learn much. Their consolation will be that any self-respecting disabled child will rapidly pick up the vibes that they're not welcome and they'll go somewhere else instead.

With a bit of luck a parent will take an obstructive setting to court under the DDA. But even then the setting needn't worry that it'll end up having to take their child! If you only open your doors because the law tells you to, nobody will want to come through them anyway. Disabled children and their families are looking for a welcome; they'll soon pick up whether that's what's on offer or not. However, the beauty of this from a provider's point of view is that you need no extra skills or knowledge to provide a welcome; just a commitment to do so.

Over and over again, when professionals approach the inclusion of disabled children with a positive 'can-do' attitude, they report that it's not such a big deal; and that even when it's demanding, the outcomes for everyone involved – staff and children (disabled and non-disabled) – are usually well worth the effort. I don't mean for a moment that it's always plain sailing, but experience suggests that even the occasional storms are worth navigating.

Reasonable adjustments or special treatment?

However, we do need to take care that our motivation for making any changes to the way we do things is driven only by a wish for fairness. Disabled people shouldn't get a special deal because they're disabled. They should get a fair deal according to what their needs may be.

Most children have an acute sense of fairness. They'll soon suss out if you're being fair or if you're giving favours. I'd suggest, for instance, that if a disabled teenager needs a personal assistant it is fair to have to pay only one entrance fee if he wants to attend some event or other. But it's a favour – and patronising – to say 'free entry for the disabled'.

This distinction between fairness and favours was neatly demonstrated by the kids at an after-school club which a disabled girl started to attend. At first she was allowed to push in to the queue for snacks. Staff recognised that they were being truly inclusive when the children started to tell her to go to the back!

In other words, she stopped getting special favours; she just got fairness. On the other hand, if her condition had meant that waiting or being in a noisy line of boisterous children would have been a genuine difficulty, then a different snack system might have been a reasonable adjustment.

So, no special favours 'because he's disabled', please. Just sensitivity to how each person's needs might be met. The child with a visual or hearing impairment may sit closer to the TV than the rest. Kids need to know why, so they can understand the exception is about fairness, not unfairness. For most children, being too close to the screen may be bad for their eyes, but if you can't see or

hear very well, being close to the screen is essential if you're going to get similar enjoyment to your non-disabled peers.

We're all different

So, to summarise this chapter, let's blow one more lurking assumption out of the water. You're pretty sure to hear someone proudly say that they treat disabled children just the same as others - 'We don't even notice he's disabled.' I know what they mean, but this is dodgy ground. If we treat our friendly vegetarian 'the same', he'll get landed with roast beef. Our blind child will go to the wrong cupboard. The lad with the hearing impairment won't hear the TV. In fact treating people 'the same' sounds like the complete opposite of making reasonable adjustments.

If what we really mean is that we'll treat everyone with the same respect, that's fine. But to do this, we'll have to respond to their differences – whoever they are, disabled or non-disabled.

Chapter 3
Who's Boris?

If you're anything like lots of other people, one of the reasons you may feel nervous about working with disabled children is the thought of all those complicated impairments they might have – and the fact that you know next to nothing about any of them. So, a word of reassurance. You won't find yourself working with 'disabled children' at all.

You will simply find yourself welcoming Boris - or Maurice, or Doris. You won't even need to know too much about the in's and out's of whatever Boris may 'have', because it's more important to focus on who you've got, rather than what he's got.

The person before the impairment

It will probably be useful to gradually gather some general information about autism or deafness or whatever. But even if you managed to clock up a training course about every different impairment under the sun, this would only be of limited value. What you need to know is not 101 things about Boris' condition, but quite a few things about Boris.

If you do get hold of an expert on Boris' condition, try to get one who knows how it affects Boris. Number one expert, of course, may well be Boris himself. Then probably his family. And then other professionals. It is Boris you'll be working with, not a condition. His impairments, whatever they may be, do not define him. They are part of who he is, and he'll respond to them quite differently from Maurice, who may have the same 'label' but is a different person.

'We had a little blind boy
last year, so

we'll
be okay
with another
blind boy'. No!
Last year Maurice; this
year Boris. Maurice didn't
mind banging into stuff and
took his life in his hands, shouted
the odds, flirted with the girls, swore
freely, liked soul music and happened to be
blind. Boris is more timid, takes no risks, speaks

quietly, barely interacts with either girls or boys, has hardly heard a swear word, enjoys Beethoven – and also happens to be blind.

All this, however, does not mean to say that you shouldn't take any notice of Boris's impairment. You absolutely must. You need to know the particular requirements that his needs place on you.

So, whilst you don't need to hold encyclopedic knowledge of whatever Boris has 'got', you do need to gather information from him, the people he lives with and maybe others who work with him at school or elsewhere.

A standard (if slightly radical) information form will probably do the trick. The key question is something like, 'What do we need to know about your child in order that we can make them welcome, ensure they feel okay here, keep them safe, and enable them to join in?' I would humbly suggest that this is a much better question than, 'Does your child have special needs?' – not least because the setting should be concerned about these things for *any* child. It's not a special question just for disabled children.

Many settings now use a scrapbook or booklet format which allows children and their families to introduce themselves with words, photos and pictures to the people who will be working with them. What makes me happy? Sad? Frightened? What sorts of help do I like to have?

Either of these methods will indicate to parents — all parents — what you think is important in your setting. And there is something else important going on too - you are telling parents (whose child may have been unwelcome elsewhere) that you want this information so that you can make sure that he gets his needs met and that he has a good time — not so that you have ammunition to exclude him, but so you have the necessary knowledge to include him.

Relationships

Do use the form or the booklet as an excuse for a conversation. It might be a good idea, especially if the requirements relating to a child are particularly complex, to go and visit him. He and his family may also want to come and have a look around first. You may want to use such a visit to ask him what he most fancies doing, enabling him to have a go at it, and asking if there's anything he'd find tricky about your setting and the way you do things. Communicate. Be interested in him. Build a relationship. Together you will find ways of doing things.

And then, during and after day one, check in with Boris

and his family to see how things are going. What's been best so far, and what's he finding difficult? Together you may decide to revise what you're doing. Ask about things. When he makes that screeching noise, is he happy or frustrated? And what should you do about it, if anything? Don't overdo it, but keep observing and keep communicating.

None of this is rocket science! You will have noticed (you did, didn't you?) that your engagement with Boris is not dominated by 'problems' or by his impairment but by whether and how he has a good time. One of the downsides of talking 'special needs' is that it constantly reinforces the mistaken idea that these kids are principally a bundle of needs. As if they had no interests, talents, skills, enthusiasms and personalities! How about focusing on these? Let's seek out these attributes and give them free rein. And whilst we are about it, can't we do that with every child, disabled or otherwise?

Communication

If you're particularly observant, you may have noticed that I didn't say 'talk to him' in the bit I've just written about relationships. I said 'communicate'. This was for two main reasons.

Firstly, speech may not work for Boris. You may need to

sign, write, gesture or whatever. Find out what Boris understands. When you think about it, you'll probably recognise that you already communicate in all sorts of different ways with children anyway – winking, smiling, fixing them with 'that look', waving your arms about, larking around. Often all you need to do is an extension of the same stuff. Sometimes you'll need to learn a more formal communication system.

Secondly, communication is not a one way process. It's just as important – maybe more important – that you listen to Boris – or attend carefully to whatever he can communicate, in whatever way he does so. He may not speak, for instance, but the fact that he's biting you could just mean that he is trying to tell you something!

He just doesn't communicate!

Communicate too with parents. It's an old cliché that

'parents are the experts on their children', to which I'd say that a parent is usually *one* of the experts on their children. They know lots, but not everything. Some of the things they do with their child may be helpful, some less helpful. Engage with them - share one another's ideas and experience.

And, just in case I've come over as dismissive of specialists in particular impairments, do engage with these professionals too. It's great to have another type

of expertise available. Specialist experts can be a huge bonus to your setting's competence and to the trust parents may place in you. Sometimes they are indispensable and will need to be in there with you and the child, at least for a while. Just be wary of any so-called expert, parent or professional, who comes with a 'can't-do' attitude. And seek out those professionals who want to share their expertise rather than keep it to themselves.

Bad risk and good risk

For a very few children, whose impairments are particularly complex or whose requirements are especially demanding, you may need to do a risk assessment focused on the child and the activities she's going to be doing. And by 'activities' I don't just mean rock-climbing and obviously risky stuff; I mean thinking through her whole day in some detail to ensure she will be okay in even the most mundane situations. Here you may well want to involve someone who has more experience than you do. But even when it is necessary and appropriate to plan in this detail — in fact, *especially* when this level of concern is required — hold in mind that the risk assessment is still only a means to a greater end. We're making sure she's safe, and that other children around her are safe, in order that she can enjoy opportunities made available to her. It's not enough that nothing untoward happens - something positive needs to happen too.

And, perversely perhaps, one of the things I'd suggest you want to plan in (as well as plan out) is risk! I was once asked by a local authority if I'd come and run a day for their Area Special Educational Needs Coordinators (incidentally, how about calling these guys Inclusion Coordinators instead? Anyway, I digress…). They wanted a session on 'risk assessment for disabled children'. I knew the training manager so I told her I'd be saying that risk is a really good thing for disabled children. 'That's why I'm asking you to do it', she replied. So, before we move on, a quick rant about risk.

We live in an increasingly risk-averse society. Playgrounds are increasingly anodyne 'in case someone gets hurt' (though statistics show that playgrounds are actually remarkably safe; if we want to address real dangers, it would be much more productive to make cars drive at 15 mph). In work with children – and the National Childcare Standards regrettably reinforce this – the aim often seems to be to eliminate risk (which is actually impossible), rather than to manage risk. What kind of practice does this give children for living in the real world? How will they learn to face risk, judge risk, embrace risk and reject risk if we remove it from their growing up – even from their play, where they could and surely should be trying out risk?

Of course we need to pay attention to major dangers, but parts of play surely should be risky (try 'challenging' or 'stretching' if the word itself is too risky!). If you visit a good inclusive adventure playground you'll see kids in bare feet running around outside; kids on trikes careering down slopes; climbers; jumpers; balancers on high-up things; kids getting particularly wet and dirty. And lots of them are children with some kind of impairment or other.

How great are the risks? Well, the odd cut foot, bumped knee, attack of wild stinging nettle perhaps. But, so long as you know that these aren't critical incidents for a particular child (and you will have found this out in advance, won't you?!), so what?

I think it's important that all children get the chance to

test themselves and try new things. For disabled children I think it's especially important. And for those whose impairments are most severe, risk remains crucial, even though they may be risking a comparatively tiny new experience. Maybe the biggest 'risk' we should be trying to avoid is actually over-protection.

Beyond reasonable adjustments

When I first started working as an inclusive play trainer I put quite a lot of emphasis on helping people to think creatively about adapting activities – 'making reasonable adjustments' if you like, even before the appearance of the DDA. This remains important, but I've been struck more recently by a different set of concerns from colleagues seeking to include disabled children.

Several years ago the few disabled children getting included in ordinary provision were usually not the most challenging to our existing ways of doing things. Quite reasonably, because this was a new way of working, they were kids who stood a decent chance of 'fitting in'. With some creative thinking we could adjust what we usually did and successfully welcome these children without radical change.

Today, though, having demonstrated that inclusion can work, some settings are starting to include children with much more complex impairments. The challenge then is to work out how we welcome and engage with children who won't benefit from our just making small adjustments to usual practice. How, for instance, do we work with children who may be lying down immobile all the time? For whom even the most imaginatively adapted form of football is still a complete impossibility? Whose behaviour seems extremely bizarre? Or who need consistent specialised medical interventions?

Making tables different heights, playing games in supportive pairs, and having paintbrushes with thicker handles might well do the trick for including some disabled children. But the challenge for other children is way beyond 'adapting activities'.

Children first

What these children demand of us is that we stop thinking, 'How can I make this activity accessible for Boris?' and start thinking of Boris first and activities second. What would Boris like to do? What does he enjoy? What might he like to try? And how could we make that possible? His pleasures may seem small to us, but that's where we're going to start. As I said in Chapter 2, for true inclusion the setting needs to fit around the child.

We also need to recognise that some people will never be able to do what others can. I work from time to time, for instance, with a trainer who happily describes the effect of her impairment as being that she wobbles. She wrily observes that she will never be a brain surgeon! That's fine by her, and it certainly doesn't mean that because she won't be a brain surgeon, nobody else should either.

But in our play settings we may be tempted to feel that we simply shouldn't do certain things if a disabled child can't join in – that if it's not appropriate for everyone, it's suspect. However, once we think about including Boris, whose capacities may seem very limited, we see how daft it would be to rule out everything Boris can't do. We'd probably end up with no children wanting to come at all – except Boris!

What I think this shows us is that inclusion is not about everyone doing the same thing all the time. It's about ensuring there are lots of different things for kids to choose from — lots of ways of engaging with things, with people and with activity. And an ethos which sees as much value in one child's enjoyment as another's - whoever the child and whatever their pleasure.

Nor should we be the arbiters of what is best for each child. For some, being with other children, at whatever level of engagement with them, will in itself be a joy. For others it may not be. We'll have to find out what suits each one. We perhaps need to see inclusion much more as a commitment to uphold each child's opportunities to do what they'd like, where they like, with whom they like, rather than trying to get them to do what we've decided they could do. This is very close to being a good definition of playwork too — just have a look at Chapter 1 of The Buskers Guide to Playwork.

Inclusion then requires that we start with each individual child and see how we can remove any barriers preventing her from doing what she wants — which is rather different from starting with a particular activity or provision and seeing whether we can adjust it so that a child can take part. For a start she may simply be unable to do it. Just as importantly, it might not even be what she wants to do!

Chapter 4
The missing children

Okay, you're convinced! Not only does it seem a good idea to welcome disabled children into your setting, but you've developed your confidence and convinced your colleagues. You've changed your publicity, advertised your inclusiveness, topped up on positive image posters and you're raring to go. So where are all the disabled kids then? Why don't they come?

Well, the reality is that history, culture, expectations and experience still conspire against you. For all the changes that are slowly taking place, most families with disabled children still don't expect them routinely to be able to go wherever they want. Even if the welcome is there and any necessary assistance can be put in place, they may not trust it.

Barriers
Partly they are themselves caught up in the 'special' culture that has grown up around disability. They've been told over and over, in subtle and not-so-subtle

ways (often starting at a time of huge emotional vulnerability when they learned that their child was not the perfect baby they'd dreamed of) that their child has 'special needs' and will need special stuff. And by and large, special provision is then exactly what families and children have been offered (if they've been offered anything at all, that is).

And then along comes another set of professionals saying, 'You don't want specialist provision! Whatever are you thinking of?! Inclusion will be best for Boris.' It's hardly surprising that there's no stampede into ordinary provision when parents may have had to fight for a

specialist service and found it to be a lifeline.

For some parents the barriers are different. One mother I met had tried to find childcare for her daughter, who has a visual impairment and learning difficulties. She rang literally dozens of places, many of whom were on record as 'taking disabled children', but none of them would have her daughter. They didn't even offer to meet her! She found herself trying to 'sell' her daughter, marketing her own child. If this happened to you, it's not difficult to see why you might decide it's not worth the hassle, the emotional bruising, of rejection. Why carry on knocking on doors when you know they'll be slammed in your face?

Other families may have tried a supposedly inclusive setting but found staff unwilling or unable to respond effectively. Sometimes this is not about a lack of commitment from the setting but the absence of appropriate support from the local authority – as advice, funding or additional staff may sometimes be required. It's pretty clear that including disabled children ineptly is worse than not including them at all. And parents who've had a negative experience are unlikely to jump at the chance to put their child and themselves through such disappointment again.

So, if you want to give disabled children the chance of coming to your setting, you're probably going to have to do something to break the cycle of expectation. If you want disabled children and their families to consider something significantly different, you're going to have to do something significantly different yourself. If you always do what you've always done, you'll always get what you've always got.

Contacting the missing children

So, go and find them! Either you, or someone working with a specific responsibility to do so, needs to go and meet disabled children and their families, tell them what you offer, invite them to visit and show them how good you are at what you do. And tell them they could come too if they like.

You can't make them come of course – always remember that inclusion is about choice. Some still won't want to shift from what has become familiar. However, if you offer a real alternative, others will probably bite your hand off - though not literally, as you'll have found out…

Trust

The key is to establish trust with the child and whoever looks after her at home. Just like any other mums, dads or carers, the parents want to feel confident that their child will be safe with you and will have a good time with you. You can show them what you already do and you can discuss with them what else might be required for their particular child. Don't be tempted to pretend that you already know; really listen to what they tell you. Professionalism is not knowing all the answers but asking enough of the right questions.

The extra adult

Sometimes you may decide that an extra adult will be needed in your setting to enable a particular child to join you there. After all that I've been going on about, you probably won't need me to tell you how you'll decide this – but I'll say it anyway. That is, you'll never need an extra member of staff just because a 'disabled child' is coming. You'll only need one if there are particular requirements relating to your inclusion of this particular child in this particular setting – and if those requirements cannot properly be met by the staff and children who are already there.

If an extra grown-up does turn out to be necessary, then everyone needs to be very clear about her role. As far as possible her job is to make herself redundant, enabling other staff and children to learn what works well for the child and enabling the disabled child himself to move away from dependency and to develop relationships with other children and adults. Anyone assisting a disabled child needs to be clear that their role is to facilitate inclusion, not just to look after him. It is all too easy to smother him or get in the way of him doing things with other kids.

A good test is to imagine what would happen if the extra adult were taken ill during the day. Could you find ways of enlisting the kids and your colleagues to enable Boris to stay? If so, you might want to ask yourself whether you really need that extra adult at all. Since inclusion is your aim, you may need to check that adults aren't actually contributing to his exclusion.

It is important to note here that occasionally – especially for some of those children with very challenging behaviour or complex impairments – a traditional 'one-to-one worker' may be exactly what's required. But be absolutely sure it's the best and only way before you ask someone to be constantly at the child's side. How would *you* like it if you were that child and it wasn't strictly necessary?

Getting the nature of any necessary assistance agreed, understood and established by the team, parent, extra adult and child, may also be a significant element in establishing the trust referred to above. Ensuring that the child and parents have a big say in who provides focused support, especially if it involves intimate care or physical handling, is another way of conferring dignity and promoting trust. And unless the child requires specialist skills that you and your team don't possess, an adult who already knows the setting and/or the child is much more likely to facilitate his inclusion than someone recruited new.

'Bridging' roles

A growing bank of evidence from around the country seems to indicate that a rather different type of 'extra adult' can be crucial in transforming good inclusive intentions into actual practice – and getting disabled children consistently into ordinary settings. This is an adult, experienced with disabled children and certainly clued up about inclusion, who acts as a bridge between child and setting.

This 'bridging' person effectively holds the family in one hand and the setting that their child wants to attend in the other. The 'bridge' acknowledges the understandable nervousness there may on both sides, providing a trusted reference and advice point for all parties, and enabling their coming together to be knowledgably supported. Most importantly, the bridge can be gradually withdrawn once everyone is working confidently together on common ground. As inclusion becomes more and more ordinary, the need for bridging roles may diminish, but at least in the early days it appears to be a vital component of many successes.

Spread good practice

With a disabled child happily settled and enjoying life in an ordinary setting, it's much more likely that others will follow. The grapevine of parents will soon be buzzing (can grapevines buzz?) and once one family has blazed a trail others will have the proof of trustworthiness they need. Attracting additional disabled children may then become much easier. In fact, you may conceivably find yourself in different difficulties – with disproportionately large numbers of disabled children wanting to join your setting because you have a reputation for such good practice.

So why could this present 'difficulties'? Because one of the benefits you offer is that you are an ordinary setting – and if you're not careful you could find your success turning you into a new specialist setting with unduly large numbers of disabled children and young people. When you start drawing disabled children from well outside your natural catchment area, it may be time to use what you have learned to help other local providers do what you've managed to do. After all, if you've moved to include disabled children, why shouldn't everyone else?

And finally......

This is the 'frequently asked questions' bit! I hope this section will tie up any loose ends for you...

What sort of training do we need?

All sorts of training can be helpful, and continually updating knowledge and skills is sure to stand you and your colleagues in good stead. Many people report, however, that one particular type of training really opens their eyes, transforms their practice and makes better sense of all the other training they do. And that is the sort of training that helps people explore and re-assess their underlying attitudes to disability and disabled children.

I hope that this book will have helped you begin to explore the attitudes you bring to the work, but there is no substitute for a high quality training course, especially if it is delivered by a skilled disabled trainer.

Aren't some disabled children better off in special schemes?

Many settings are not historically geared up for disabled children, either physically or attitudinally. And it is certainly true that some children may require very significant changes to the ways in which provision has usually been offered. Sometimes money is required; more usually a genuine commitment is required (a commitment which, in some instances, also seems to unlock the extra cash).

I believe it is possible for meaningful inclusion to be achieved for every disabled child, but current levels of understanding, organisation, and - yes — funding, may mean it will be difficult for some settings with some children until more people at both policy and practitioner level are truly committed to this agenda.

Where caring, supportive specialist services are the only ones prepared to welcome disabled children, it will of course be unlikely that those kids will start accessing ordinary settings. Indeed, it would be irresponsible to encourage them to do so. Just as irresponsible, in fact, as denying them the means to choose the option of taking part successfully in any local provision they'd like to…..

What words aren't we allowed to use (this week)?

The question of appropriate terminology in relation to disability issues is a thorny one. But it does not deserve to be ridiculed and dismissed as 'political correctness'. I frequently hear that one phrase or another is supposedly 'in' or 'out', 'flavour of the month' or something 'they' (whoever they are) say we shouldn't use. But the words we use do convey messages – that's what words are for! – and different words will therefore send different messages.

The key principles with terminology are to choose words that are

(i) factually accurate - which rules out things like 'able-bodied', because lots of disabled people are able-bodied too, and

(ii) faithful reflections of what you believe – which, amongst other things (you won't be surprised to learn by now!), rules out 'special' as far as I am concerned.

You may have noticed that I've referred throughout this book to 'children with impairments'. This is because I wish to put the child first rather than their condition. I also consistently refer to 'disabled children'. This is because I wish to reinforce my belief that children may

60

have their impairments but that they are disabled by our responses to them. Given this understanding, it does not make logical sense for me to talk about 'children with disabilities', since the child may 'have' the impairment but is disabled by the rest of us and the world he lives in.

For further guidance about language, the National Childminding Association has a really useful handout ('Word power') in its CD-Rom for trainers ('Inclusive Childminding') - details can be found in the bibliography.

What if other children take the mickey?

Use the policies you would use for handling any child being unpleasant to another child. First, support the child on the receiving end; second, talk with the perpetrator. On the whole, if you explain things to non-disabled children from the outset, they are less likely to take the mick, especially if they have routinely grown up alongside disabled children from their earliest years.

What do I do if non-disabled children's parents object or threaten to withdraw their children?

Firstly, don't assume the critics are prejudiced. They may be, but they may be quite legitimately concerned that in your laudable desire to be fair to disabled children, you are actually being unfair to the rest! Are you managing the inclusion of disabled children in a way that significantly disadvantages one or more non-disabled children?

Only after you've taken a good look at what you're

doing and re-assessed your practice can you start thinking about prejudice as the basis for a complaint. Even then, treat any complainant with concern and respect – they may have genuine fears. Help them understand your setting's commitment to inclusion and equality of opportunity – and, if necessary, point out your legal responsibilities under the DDA.

If they still won't shift, they'll probably take their child and their discriminatory attitudes elsewhere. And with a bit of luck they'll keep hearing the same message and have to consider whether it's they themselves who are out of step, rather than you.

Have I got to take disabled children?

What you've 'got' to do is make those 'reasonable adjustments'. If you discuss everything you might do with child, family and colleagues and reach the conclusion together that you cannot currently arrange things to ensure the well-being of the disabled child and other children, you are not breaking the law by deciding that she cannot come. In fact, pretending that you can make a child sufficiently safe and welcome when you can't is a sure fire way of getting inclusion a bad name. Referring the child to colleagues who can help her and her parents/carers find a viable alternative should be the least you would do. Such assistance should automatically follow if your genuine 'can-do' attitude has regretfully come up with a 'can't do here at the moment' end result.

Who pays if it's going to cost more?

This is a 'biggy'! Firstly, check the assumption. Very often it doesn't cost more to include a disabled child. If it really does in a particular instance, though, the answers are not laid down.

For those settings where fees are paid, one option is to set all charges higher from the outset, to ensure money is saved and available when needed for particular children. This might sound equitable, but it is likely to alienate your regulars and/or price yourself out of the market. Neither of which is an especially good idea!

Sometimes the family itself is asked to pay extra (though the DDA says the increased cost of providing a service can only be charged to the user if it goes beyond 'reasonable adjustments' and becomes a 'tailor-made service' - and even an additional adult is not usually seen as a tailor-made service). Whilst money from 'direct payments' (state cash to disabled children's families in place of designated service provision) could legitimately be used to pay for additional costs, arguments rage as to whether it is appropriate for other disability benefits to meet such charges – especially as families with disabled children are